SEVENTIESTYLE

home decoration and furnishings from the 1970s

PUBLISHED BY MIDDLESEX UNIVERSITY PRESS

CONTENTS

INTRODUCTION

'That doesn't mean, of course, that the pound here in Britain – in your pocket or purse or in your bank – has been devalued' opined Sir Harold Wilson, announcing the devaluation of the pound in November 1967. In the subsequent decade, problems in the economy and widespread crises in the delivery of Wilson's self-proclaimed 'technological age' created a symptomatic insecurity in culture.

Throughout the 70s the pound in your pocket was being replaced by the credit on your card (introduced in 1970); the 70s felt plentiful but insecure. In architecture and design the decade was marked by a simultaneous and dynamic exploration of the potential of new materials, technologies and processes in some sectors of design while in others there was an equally dynamic reclamation of the past and exploration of the traditions of other cultures.

Essex Design Guide,
Essex County Council, 1973
The Essex Design Guide *proposed to do away with the perceived evil of the suburb by getting rid of how it looked and substituting either a pronounced urban density and appearance for new developments based on small towns or a rural 'look' based on the appearance of villages.*

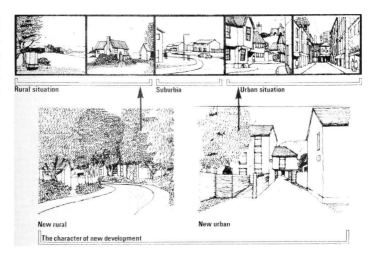

Rural situation   Suburbia   Urban situation

New rural   New urban

The character of new development

Ideal Home, September 1977
South Woodham Ferrers, a small New Town (1975) was
the first housing development built under the aegis of the
Essex Design Guide for Residential Areas. Criticised by
some as 'a passport to Noddyland' the design guide set
the standard for the majority of housing developments
since its publication in 1973. Its recommendations
combined the statistically proven preference of the public
for traditional house forms and building materials with
designs that accommodated a wide range of dwelling
sizes that reflected new demographic trends, particularly
the increase in small households, and estate layouts that
were good for both cars and pedestrians.

In housing this is represented by the contrast between the use of highly expressive Brutalist architecture for housing by some local authorities in the early years of the decade and the almost simultaneous development of a complete volte face in other parts of the public sector. This is best represented by the *Essex Design Guide for Residential Areas* (1973), a publication as influential on public and private housing of the 70s as the Parker Morris report of the early 60s. Its proposals favoured a return to the rural-inspired neo-vernacular architecture and planning that dominated domestic architecture before the bold Modernism of the 50s and 60s. Demographic and economic changes brought about the decrease in the dominance of medium-sized family housing in favour of a greater diversity of housing types from very small to very large. However, they all shared in the increasing provision of insulation, central heating, utility spaces and multiple bath and toilet facilities. Houses of the 70s also increasingly abandoned open planning in favour of multiple reception rooms.

In the 70s the population grew by only 405,000 compared to the 60s total growth of 2,658,000. However, there was a disproportionate growth in the number of households which had increased by 20 per cent by the end of the 70s compared to 1961 levels, although the population had only grown by 7 per cent over the same period. Total house building declined by 50 per cent over the decade while at the same time home ownership increased and reduced renting to about 11 per cent of the housing stock.

Underlying these changes was a greater preparedness in the population to own older properties for a combination of pragmatic and aesthetic reasons. Equally the Government began to recognise the economic sense of repairing and modernising older property and with a number of Acts, starting in 1969, began to subsidise rehabilitation of existing buildings. This had the effect of greatly increasing the interest in, and work undertaken, on older houses of inner-city suburbs, like Islington, and disused farm buildings in the country. This in turn started the market in conversions and additions that is such a feature of the contemporary middle-class housing market as well as stimulating what were later termed 'heritage' designs.

The rapid development of consumerism, the values of the supermarket and the boutique as applied to cars and homes, meant that the new technologies of production were applied with more and more ruthless economy to an ever wider range of domestic products creating cheaper, more self-consciously stylish, transient and undurable things – homes may have had more baths but they were often plastic. The growing insecurity amongst consumers about the future in its widest sense led

Golden Homes, 1977
This shows a converted barn (1977) in the Cotswolds. An innovation in the housing market of the 70s was the conversion of derelict farm buildings into homes. In early conversions like this, standardised building elements like hardwood siding and metal framed 'standard' windows were used with designs that took as their model Modern houses. Later, as the market became more aware of issues around preservation and conservation, conversions were often designed to work within and be sympathetic to the original structure, materials and form of the building.

some into a nostalgic hunt for authenticity using the 'pick and mix' methods of the fancy dress party.

Designers, trained as Modernists in the new Art School culture of the 60s and early 70s, conflated a fundamental belief in Modern design with a creative process derived from fashion. This, in combination with the trend in popular culture toward the reclamation of earlier styles like Art Nouveau and Art Deco and an interest in alternative non-urban, non-western design cultures, led to a strange combination of designs which were fundamentally Modernist but simultaneously overlaid with the auras of glamorous urban pasts, bountiful rural cosiness or an exotic ethnic location. These 'themed' designs, frequently articulated in the same location like Barbara Hulanicki's Biba department store in Knightsbridge or the Sunday magazines, encapsulated the fantasies of the grown up 60s generation who now consumed interior design as they had learnt to buy fashion. This diverse and heterogeneous taste meant that there emerged interior designs which began to display different narratives almost from room to room in a manner that now is recognised in the terms 'themeing' or 'lifestyle'. The 70s was a decade when consumerism, fashion and technology combined to create an interior design culture that encouraged individuals to give form to their daydreams.

FURNITURE

In fashionable homes of the early 70s there was a desire to do away with most conventional furniture and replace it with upholstered areas covered in rich and exotic fabrics like furs, kelims or Indian prints. There was a fashion for anti-furniture like Zanotta's 'Sacco', a sort of tailored bean bag and Panton's experiments with soft womblike 'environments' within rooms. Italian designers perfected the most enduringly popular of 70s furniture types, the soft, low modular sofa that could be added together to fit around almost any space like the architectural fashion for sunken living rooms. Another was the huge, low bed on a dais. Coffee tables assumed a greater importance than in previous decades and were larger, lower and squarer than their predecessors, combining rich materials like marble, rosewood or bevelled plate glass supported by bronze, gold-plated or lacquered brass legs.

Dining furniture followed this theme of luxury, though transparent materials and thin sections were often used to reduce its 'presence'. With the development of vacuum-moulded ABS plastic the Italians also developed ranges of highly coloured shiny plastic tables and chairs, like Magistretti's Selene chair which could function anywhere, indoors or out.

At the top of the market, and the student-improvised bottom, there was a progressive interest in the rural and the handcrafted. For the less well off this was expressed through the purchase of old country furniture, iconically the pine kitchen table. At the upper end designers like John Makepeace created furniture from native hardwoods that were often very large.

In Britain the most important retailer was Terence Conran's Habitat. In the 70s Conran recognised consumerism as the driving force behind aesthetics and Habitat offered a range of styles that fitted the 'mood' of the buyer. This concept was clearly described in his House Book. Modern was reduced to a 'look' alongside other styles that reflected the eclectic nostalgia that was fashionable in the 70s.

ILLUSTRATION I
The Architectural Review, August 1973

Reproduced courtesy of OMK Design

ILLUSTRATION I Many Modernist designers of the 70s ceased to design for the domestic market as there was greater creative freedom and more money to be made in contract furnishing. This quickly led the consumer to link Modern design of this kind with the workplace rather than the home. This gradually eroded the taste for 'functional Modernism' in the consumer.

ILLUSTRATION 2 As system furniture grew in popularity and sophistication, sofa designers began to design system sofas that would adapt to any room layout. These quickly superseded the old three piece suite before falling from favour in the late 70s.

ILLUSTRATION 2
The House Book, Terence Conran, 1974

© Camera Press

ILLUSTRATION 3
Advertisement from House and Garden, *March 1979*

ILLUSTRATION 3 Throughout the 70s there was a reappraisal of earlier decades of the century. This led to a new taste in design classics and the emergence of a 'top 100 designs' mentality at the upper end of the market. Here furniture is exhibited like art – contemporary designs are framed by classics from earlier in the century.

ILLUSTRATION 4

Advertisement from Ideal Home, *March 1974*

ILLUSTRATION 5

Ideal Home, *January 1976*

ILLUSTRATION 6

Ideal Home, *January 1976*

ILLUSTRATION 7

Advertisement from Homes and Gardens, *October 1974*

ILLUSTRATION 4 This suite by Schreiber was looking very dated despite the contemporary styling of elements like the mirrors and stool.

ILLUSTRATIONS 5 & 6 From the late 60s there was a growing fashion for reclaiming everyday antique furniture. This went hand in hand with the developing taste for the 'natural' which led to the fashion for stripping this furniture of its original paint finishes and then polishing the pine wood beneath.

ILLUSTRATION 7 Built-in furniture reached its apogee in the early 70s with the attempt by system furniture manufacturers to latch on to the idea of environment design. This bedroom design furnishes the entire room – all that need be added are personal details.

Photographer: Jessica Strang

ILLUSTRATION 8
The House Book, *Terence Conran, 1974*

ILLUSTRATION 8 In the 60s a lot of attention was given to design for children. Throughout the 70s those children, now teenagers, were concerned to express their individuality by decorating for themselves and their rooms became the no-go areas they are today. Teenagers typically used found objects and the printed ephemera of pop culture to decorate their rooms — sticky labels, posters and junk were all used to make the objects given to them by their parents their own. This room shows childhood bunks lying beneath a sediment of Donny Osmond material while a Chopper, designed specifically for teenagers, lies near a hand-me-down but desirable 1960s Braun record player.

ILLUSTRATION 9 By the beginning of the 70s two decades of Modernism had made manufacturers and the public much more ready to accept new designs and materials. In the early 70s the consumer seems to have been prepared to accept more challenging designs than during the 60s. This middle-market suite mixes some traditional styling with ideas and materials taken from contemporary Italian design.

ILLUSTRATION 9
Advertisement from Homes and Gardens,
January & February 1971

ILLUSTRATION 10

The House Book, *Terence Conran, 1974*

ILLUSTRATION 10 The sexual revolution of the 60s was acted out more fully in the 70s and there was a greater permissiveness in ideas about sex not found today. This extreme example shows an environment style of room-sized furniture which might today be called a media room – here it is a 'seduction pad' with tape deck and film projector close by the sofa bed.

ILLUSTRATION 11

Advertisement from Ideal Home,
March 1974

ILLUSTRATION 11 By the 70s modularised built-in furniture was widely accepted. Its principles began to be applied to furnishing living areas and this led to the gradual disappearance of the sideboard in favour of wall units which could also function as room dividers.

FURNISHING FABRICS

In the 70s there was a more widespread use of synthetic materials and economic printing methods. Curtain fabrics tended to be lighter in weight than equivalent fabrics of the 60s. By contrast, early 70s upholstered furniture used some heavy and unconventional fabrics, like elephant cord, in either creams or very rich colours influenced by late 60s clothing fashions.

The large curtain patterns of the 60s were replaced by bright, geometric patterns in the early 70s. By the middle of the decade, Modernist fabric designs were being replaced by a wide range of design options – Modern, 'ethnic' and nostalgic – reflecting the stylistic eclecticism of the decade.

Metropolitan taste favoured various types of minimalist approach. At one extreme there was a taste for replacing curtains with white blinds, roman, jalousie, luxaflex or roller, at the other a taste for glamorous furnishings in fabrics like satins and velvets. At a more national level there was a style for combining thin, pale translucent curtains with plain or elegantly printed roller blinds and furniture in large repeat patterns.

The main stylistic innovation was a return to historicism. In the early part of the decade there was a strong interest in popular cultures and styles of the early 20th century, reflected in Art Nouveau and Deco-inspired designs which could be expensively glamorous or crudely printed on cheap cotton. These cheaper designs were popular with the young, and available through shops like Habitat. The revival of interest in historic buildings led to 'historic' patterns produced by up-market design companies like Osborne and Little. These were usually small pattern repeats in a restricted range of matching colours. A popular promoter of this style was Laura Ashley, whose products became a ruralist, romantic alternative to Habitat. As with other aspects of interiors in the 70s though, modern was often combined with traditional, different themes being used from room to room.

ILLUSTRATION I

Advertisement from Homes and Gardens, October 1972

ILLUSTRATION I The huge variety of styles and patterns here share a tendency to highly coloured and simple designs that show the contemporary influence of popular graphic design on household textiles in the early 70s. The graduates of the new art schools enabled manufacturers to be much more fashionable than had been the case in the 60s.

ILLUSTRATION 2 This cheaply produced pattern picked up on the nostalgic taste for old popular cultural crafts that were seen as a local equivalent to 'ethnic' crafts. The popular crafts were a part of the countercultural ethos of the 60s student generation as they suggested a non-materialistic design tradition, though this was soon seamlessly appropriated by consumerism.

ILLUSTRATION 2

Habitat patchwork fabric, mid 1970s

ILLUSTRATION 3
The House Book, *Terence Conran, 1974*

ILLUSTRATION 4
Advertisement from Homes and Gardens, *October 1974*

ILLUSTRATION 3 The great contribution of 70s designs to Modernist architecture was colour.

Here, a Modernist living space with its 'conversation pit', which in earlier schemes would have relied on lighting and form for its contemporaneity, is transformed from architectural uptightness by a synthetic coloured 'Op-Tartan' carpet and matching purple table and sofa with contrasting apple green 'coachlining'. This strongly coloured and patterned interior

shows how adventurous the taste of the early part of the decade could be in comparison to both earlier and later decades.

ILLUSTRATION 4 The ever popular floral print became a dense carpet of flowers in designs throughout the decade. Duvets, which appeared early in the decade, were covered in curtain-style designs following the fashion for co-ordination that dominated the first two-thirds of the decade.

ILLUSTRATION 5
Advertisement from House and Garden, *October 1975*

Very Peter Hall, very Sanderson.

Sanderson

Curtains: AL 1138/1 100% wild silk (handwoven in India). Blinds: AF 540/7 cotton print.
Seats: HV 4712 colours 14 and 15 Acrylic pile (Dralon) upholstery velvet. Suede on Bookcase: 86Y2412 Canovar Suede.

Reproduced courtesy of The Sanderson Archive

ILLUSTRATION 5 While the picture window, roller blind and comfy chair in upholstered foam all suggest modern, the other furnishings, floral patterns and warm-toned plains all suggest traditional. Throughout the 70s, a confusion between modern form and traditional patterns typified the ambivalence of the decade, as both tradition and modernity offered comforts that each on its own could not fulfil.

ILLUSTRATION 6 This Sanderson advertisement epitomises the great leap backwards that occurred in interior design at the end of the 70s. Co-ordinated papers and fabrics, also provided more cheaply by Laura Ashley, allowed the public to return to a more secure Little England as economic and political crises sapped the public of its earlier passion for the future.

mentary wallpapers and fabrics from the new Chintz collection: designs "Trellis" and "Honeysuckle Trellis."
Sanderson and Sons Ltd., Sanderson House, Berners Street, London W1.

ILLUSTRATION 7
The House Book, *Terence Conran, 1974*

ILLUSTRATION 7 With the popularity of travel came the long-lasting fashion for eclectic styles of fabric that reflected other cultures and periods. Here the rococo splendour of a bedspread and a rug show how flexible the eclectic styles of the early 70s could be.

ILLUSTRATION 8 At the beginning of the decade there was a transition from the 'pop' floral designs of the 60s toward a re-evaluation of more traditional floral patterns. This pattern on a furnishing fabric represents a crossover between the two styles that disappeared early in the decade.

ILLUSTRATION 8
Linen union floral pattern on blue background, 1970

WALLS AND PAINT

The unified look of many 1960s interiors was replaced by a more individual approach to wall decoration. Brilliant white paint was still popular but less dominant. As the decade came to a close, the most ubiquitous wall paint colour was magnolia. Experiments in reflective wall surfaces were a feature of early-70s decorative schemes whereas the beginnings of a rejection of gloss woodwork in favour of flatter tones characterised the historicist schemes of the second half of the 70s.

A taste for dark secondary colours in earth or synthetic tones, particularly orange and purple, green, lacquer red, Chinese yellow and navy blue, dominated the first half of the decade. However, from about 1973, there was a growing interest in pastel colours as the romanticism of schemes suitable for historic styles became more popular. In the early 70s, glamorous schemes, often dark, glossy and theatrically lit, reflected an interest in Orientalist exoticism and Art Deco. These frequently used shiny foil-based papers and areas of mirror as well as glossy

tesserae tiling. There was also some experimentation with using heavy fabrics to cover walls.

In more modest homes, foil papers enjoyed a brief vogue to make a highlight of minor areas. Floral wallpapers began to employ naturalistic designs with a tight, large repeat. These intense patterns, like foil papers, were best used to highlight one wall in a room.

The gentrification of old houses brought about an increase of what has been called Laura Ashley style. This was based on total room schemes featuring the new wallpaper and fabric collections that enabled the homeowner to create a co-ordinated look. These 'whole room' schemes relied on pastel-toned backgrounds to small, traditional patterns that were the opposite of cosmopolitan, Deco-inspired glamour. Woodchip papers and 'artex' textured paint were often used to rescue rough surfaces in secondary rooms. In principal rooms painted, anaglypta-type papers could be used to give a more architectural reclamation to a poor surface.

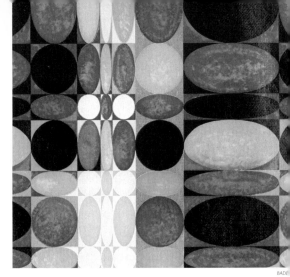

ILLUSTRATION 2
Mayfair shiny patterned wallpaper, 1978

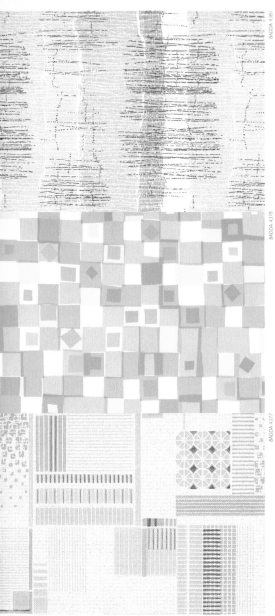

ILLUSTRATION I
Wallpapers, early 1970s

ILLUSTRATION I All these papers were bought from Kingsway Wallpaper Stores in the early years of the 70s and represent an average three-bedroomed house's wallpaper patterns. They share a bland anaemic style with small patterns and an etiolated modernist look that is more 50s than 70s in feel.

ILLUSTRATION 2 Wallpapers using metallic foils transformed the geometric Op Art papers of the late 60s into a new glamorous Modernism, more futuristic and sexy than rational and technological. They enjoyed a brief vogue and were often used in small confined spaces rather than on a large scale.

ILLUSTRATION 4

Homes and Gardens, *February 1974*

ILLUSTRATION 3 The middle of the decade was a point of collision between a new traditionalism and an earlier design environment where nostalgic and exotic themes were seen through the lens of Modern interpretation. These factors, combined with a more developed consumerist attitude, meant that wallpaper manufacturers tried to keep up with this very eclectic market by offering all the styles in all the colours.

ILLUSTRATION 4 These wallpaper patterns of the early 70s show the unique density of colour and pattern, combined with very simple repeats of the period, that created what could be called a 'psychedelic Deco' style. These patterns were too strong to be used on all four walls except, surprisingly, in small rooms.

ILLUSTRATION 3

Advertisement from Homes and Gardens, *April 1975*

ILLUSTRATION 5

The House Book, Terence Conran, 1974

Photographer: Roger Gain

ILLUSTRATION 5 One of the effects of the 'counterculture' belief that there was always an alternative was the adoption by some architects of anti-rectangular designs, based on the ideas of Rudolph Steiner or the many ethnic building traditions that use non-linear forms.

ILLUSTRATION 6

The House Book, Terence Conran, 1974

Reproduced courtesy of The Estate of David Hicks

ILLUSTRATION 6 David Hicks was an early exponent of the revival of decorative schemes based on historic styles. Here, a very 70s orange is used in homage to the decorative style of the smaller 18th-century town house that was so popular in the 80s and early 90s.

ILLUSTRATION 7 Textured wallpapers, fabrics and even carpet were used as wall coverings in schemes of the early 70s. This image shows that some DIY books were still promoting schemes that were redolent of the late 50s and early 60s despite using contemporary ideas.

Reproduced Courtesy JR Crown Paints

Reproduced courtesy of Lutterworth Press

ILLUSTRATION 8
Let's Decorate Together, Kitty Grime, 1975

Reproduced courtesy of Lutterworth Press

ILLUSTRATION 8 Textured plaster and paint products were popular with DIY enthusiasts as a way of dealing with cracks and uneven walls. Often they were used in a clumsy attempt to create 'old-fashioned' finishes as part of an 'olde-worlde' style for a cottage for example. Toward the end of the decade these products fell from favour as more authentic finishes became better known.

ILLUSTRATION 9 Although this advertisement dates from 1977, the dense supergraphic floral pattern is more representative of the advanced tastes of the early 70s. By 1977 this design in washable vinyl was too brash, psychedelic and plastic for the easy nostalgic romantic floral styles popular by then. In many respects, interior design of the 70s had adopted the transient ethos of fashion and many manufacturers found it hard to keep up.

ILLUSTRATION 10

Advertisement from Homes and Gardens, August 1978

ILLUSTRATION 10 The chemistry of paints became more sophisticated in the 70s, allowing brighter, harder and more stable colours. These were fashionable in the early 70s.

ILLUSTRATION 11 & 12 The early 70s favoured strong colours and exotic patterns, particularly those with a Mediterranean 'feel' which could suggest heat and travel.

ILLUSTRATION 11

Advertisement from Homes and Gardens, February 1977

ILLUSTRATION 12

Advertisement from Homes and Gardens, July 1974

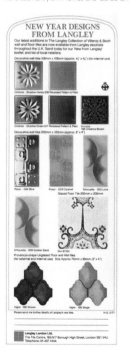

FLOORING

Cheaper manufacturing made wall-to-wall carpeting the most common flooring material of the 70s. The 'safest' choice was a Berber in flecked oatmeal, combining fashionable values like texture and naturalness. That said, the early 70s produced some bold carpet designs, picking up on the psychedelic patterns of the late 60s. Floral patterns were large and densely grouped, some reflecting the Art Deco revival early in the decade. In expensively furnished homes, richly toned Wiltons were popular. Elsewhere, increased consumerism meant that even vivid purple carpets were available following the fashion for that colour early in the decade.

Parquet floor was replaced in architect-designed homes by 'Brutalist' materials like dark brown 'Ruabon' tiles and blue semi-engineering brick. Oblong ceramic floor tiles in white and primary colours were also fashionable for kitchens and bathrooms, often rising part way up the wall. In developments with concrete floors, like the Barbican in London, carpet was also laid up the wall. For those who couldn't afford ceramic tiles, there was

the new vinyl flooring on carpet-width rolls. These were often patterned to appear like old 'Spanish' tiles or 'Italian terrazzo'. With vinyl, the dominant colours were blacks, whites, terracottas or beiges, following the fashion for wheat-coloured kitchens. Pirelli developed rubber flooring that was used extensively in the high-tech homes of the late 70s. Patterned with raised discs, it came in colours that reflected the Italian fashion for grass greens, lemon yellows and pillar box reds, as well as white.

With the popularity of doing up old houses, it became fashionable to reveal old flooring materials like deal boards and quarry tiles. Wooden floors were stripped then varnished or repainted in bright modern colours. With the move to hard floor surfaces there developed a fashion for rugs and kelims from the Middle East. Fashionable households favoured rich, long-haired carpets, though this relic of countercultural attitudes disappeared in the later 70s with the growing interest in historical British styles.

ILLUSTRATION 1
Ideal Home, January 1975

ILLUSTRATION 2
Advertisement from The Architectural Review, January 1973

ILLUSTRATION 1 Pirelli's rubber flooring was not cheap and didn't come on wide rolls, but it was very fashionable among the design conscious and was available in colours that matched Italian designs of the early and mid 70s.

ILLUSTRATION 2 Hard-wearing carpet tiles were developed in the 70s for use in areas of mixed wear so that only worn tiles need be replaced. This idea used new manufacturing processes and plastic materials that could ensure

Photographer: Jerry Tubby

ILLUSTRATION 3
The House Book, Terence Conran, 1974

ILLUSTRATION 4
The House Book, Terence Conran, 1974

consistency of colour and pile. More a product one would expect of the 60s than the fantasist 70s, they were nonetheless popular with Brutalist architects and other technocrats.

ILLUSTRATION 3 In the early 70s, the popularity of the idea of the overland route to India, of things simple and tribal in what had been the counterculture, created a market and a taste amongst young homeowners – not so much for the classic Persian rug but for the bags and flat weaves of tribal cultures from Turkey to India. These were the basis for becushioned arrangements that recalled the Orientalism of the early twentieth century and could also be seen in contemporary advertisements for Fry's Turkish Delight.

ILLUSTRATION 4 Contrast was a popular interior design technique of the early 70s as was a more general interest in sensation. Here, a white shiny vinyl floor contrasts with cream flokatis.

ILLUSTRATION 5
The House Book, *Terence Conran, 1974*

ILLUSTRATION 5 The rediscovery and renovation of Victorian and Georgian houses in the 70s was concerned with modernising the old rather than recreating it. One way of getting rid of the old darkness in these houses was by stripping and polishing their floors and this became the most fashionable floor style of the 70s.

ILLUSTRATION 6 Stripes and strongly contrasting colours were considered very chic in the first half of the 70s and were part of the interest in Art Deco that emerged at that time.

ILLUSTRATION 6
The Architectural Review, *October 1972*

ILLUSTRATION 7
The House Book, Terence Conran, 1974

ILLUSTRATION 7 Late Modernism was very sophisticated and less rationalist than earlier manifestations of the style. Gardens in the 70s were often conceived as outside rooms and, to emphasise this, the owners of this house have made the interior floor appear as a grass-like surface in contrast to the stone 'floor' of the garden.

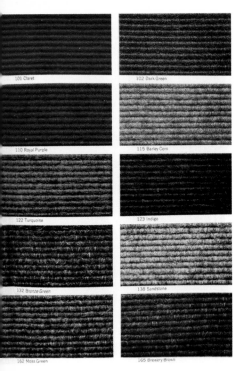

101 Claret

102 Dark Green

110 Royal Purple

115 Barley Corn

122 Turquoise

123 Indigo

132 Bronze Green

138 Sandstone

162 Moss Green

165 Brewery Brown

ILLUSTRATION 8

Advertisement from The Architectural Review, April 1972

Hutchli Bokhara finely-knotted carpet of wool and goat's hair made in the Bokhara region of Russia. The Hutchli (cross) pattern is one used throughout the Orient. The background colour is traditionally red, signifying happiness.

The Afghanistan Kelim is a tapestry-woven rug traditionally used for wall-hangings or bed covers, but they are quite sturdy enough to use as floor coverings. This Kelim, or prayer rug, is coarsely woven from a fairly harsh, thick wool.

The Kurdish Kelim is more brightly coloured than the Afghan version, the wool used is softer and glossier, and the designs are embroidered.

Berber rug from the Sahara. A woven rug in which the design for the most part adheres to stripes. The wool lacks the high gloss of the Persian rugs.

Iraqi rug, similar in design and texture to the Kurdish Kelim.

Figga rug, from Iraq, another example of geometrically-patterned Kelim rugs made mainly in muted colours.

Ethiopian rug – a coarse, woven rug. The triangles in the design are an Abyssinian symbol of happiness.

Beni Menel. A flat-woven rug made in the Lower Atlas mountain area of Morocco by Bedouin nomads. These rugs were originally designed as wall hangings and floor coverings for the nomads' tents and made useful camel blankets when the tribe was on the move. The outstanding features are the highly-stylised geometric patterns in sharp, contrasting colours.

Dhurry: The ubiquitous, hand-made Indian cotton woven rug in bright stripes. Used for wall hangings, bed and sofa covers as well as floor rugs.

Rya shaggy pile Finnish carpet (now machine-made). This example is hand-made, designed by Peter Collingwood.

Peruvian woven rug of traditional South American design – a smiling yellow sun and orange sun rays.

Mexican serape. A coarsely woven rug with fringed ends. Traditionally, this kind of fabric was made for wearing, in the form of ponchos.

(Opposite) An extravaganza of oriental patterns and colours combine to give this room a rich, warm unity.

ILLUSTRATION 9

The House Book, Terence Conran, 1974

ILLUSTRATION 8 These non-woven corded carpets, in the dark strong colours of the early 70s, reflect the persistence of Modernist styles from the 60s that, by the 70s, had become a tradition to react against.

ILLUSTRATION 9 Kelims were the new Persian rugs of the 70s. They combined the intricacy of the traditional rug with a vibrant colour and simple weave that appealed to the interest in 'ethnic' popular culture that characterised the 'magic bus' generation who now owned homes.

LIGHTING

Throughout the 60s the problem of lighting was providing even, bright illumination. By contrast, and perhaps as a reaction, the dominant style of the early 70s was one of illuminated darkness. There were few technical innovations in lighting in the 70s but there was a move toward smaller light sources. In 1972, Artemide produced the Tizio adjustable desk-lamp, designed by Richard Sapper, which used the new halogen bulb in place of the older larger tungsten bulb. By the mid 70s, spot lamps had reduced in size too. Another innovation, though at the top end of the market, was the use of groups of dimmer switches.

In retrospect, the early 70s seems a period of baroque experimentation with theatrical light effects in the home. Small electric light sources were used in dark interiors with the light modulated not only by shades but also by the reflectiveness of the surrounding surfaces using mirrors, metallic foils or very high gloss paint.

In kitchen lighting there were also few technical innovations; instead more care was taken with the creation of mood. Functional light needs were restricted to work surfaces and other 'themed' lights, like reconditioned oil lamps, were used to confer on the kitchen whatever atmosphere was desired.

There was a greater consciousness of the effect of restricting daylight by blinds, shutters, screens or nets. Architects became more experimental by moving away from large windows everywhere, toward designs that placed small or narrow windows in places between the major fenestration to provide more subtle effects with daylight. They also experimented more with clerestory windows and skylights.

The later 70s approached lighting in a calmer manner. With the growing interest in 'heritage' styles and the easy provision of more electrical power points, side lamps, uplighters and downlighters made the central ceiling lamp unfashionable unless it were a chandelier. The second half of the 70s created a market for an enormous range of different lamp designs, new and historic.

© Camera Press

ILLUSTRATION 1
The House Book, *Terence Conran, 1974*

ILLUSTRATION 1 Lighting effects became much more carefully calculated as light sources became more varied in the 70s. In kitchens, low level strip lights were used to provide useful light to work by, while low-wattage pendant lights created more atmospheric pools of light in areas where food was displayed or eaten.

ILLUSTRATION 2 In the 1970s, kitchens became as much a site of narration as living rooms or bedrooms. Lighting became a major signifier of theme and usually this task was borne by the central light fitting which was more decorative than necessary. This image shows how a rattan lampshade could contribute to the long-lasting fashion of the farmhouse look.

ILLUSTRATION 3 This iconic image of comfortable 1970s London shows, incidentally, the light effects created by shutters, which were rediscovered early in the decade.

ILLUSTRATION 2
Homes and Gardens, *February 1975*

Photographer John Miller Reproduced courtesy of IPC Media

ILLUSTRATION 3

Mr and Mrs Clark and Percy, David Hockney, 1970-71

ILLUSTRATION 4 This room shows a great variety of 70s lighting effects in an architecture designed with dramatic lighting in mind. The light from the clerestory windows illuminates much of the room though diffused by a woven screen. In the ceiling below, recessed downlighters fill the space between the clerestory light and the abundant side-lamps whose shades angle light down into pools below eye level and, in smaller amounts, upward to light a framed print. A picture window provides a brighter light level for a side chamber to the main space.

ILLUSTRATION 4

House and Garden, *December & January, 1979-80*

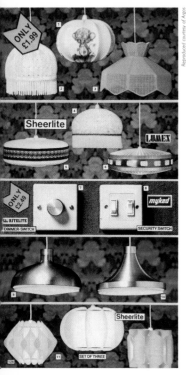

ILLUSTRATION 5
Argos catalogue, 1977

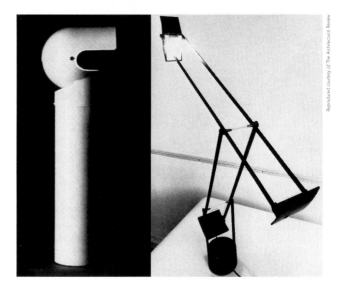

ILLUSTRATION 6
The Architectural Review, December 1972

ILLUSTRATION 5 Of all the variations on the pendant light shown here, the most popular were numbers one, two and three from the Argos catalogue, perhaps because they were cosy rather than assertively modern.

ILLUSTRATION 6 Gae Aulenti's Pileo lamp represents the sculptural minimalism of early 70s Italian design though it is fundamentally still only a light bulb. Richard Sapper's Tizio lamp was a radical transformation of the old Anglepoise through the use of the much more intense and concentrated white light given by the tiny halogen bulb in its first successful domestic design application.

FINISHING TOUCHES

Earlier in the century, finishing touches to a home almost certainly meant pictures, photographs, ornamental pottery and possibly some type of plant. By the 1970s, the status-affirming purchases were the products of new technologies, particularly electronics.

In the 70s, consumerism accelerated and American-style 'affluence' products appeared. People began to own more cars, which affected the space around a house – gardens being given over to parking. New houses often had double garages as a statement of wealth. Swimming pools appeared in back gardens at the cost of lawns. Indoors, homes increasingly had two or more bathrooms or added en-suite facilities to bedrooms. Televisions not only grew larger but also smaller for bedrooms and kitchens. Multiple telephones became more common and radios were either part of the hi-fi or small and portable.

More traditional finishing touches, like dinner services and silver-plate canteens, became less popular as they could be damaged by dishwashers. They were replaced by new ranges of dishwasher safe oven-to-tableware, combining the aesthetics of show pottery with the durability of kitchenware.

There were many transient fashions, like macramé plant holders and folding screens in bedrooms, but the most significant 70s finishing touch was hi-fi. Expensive in the 60s, hi-fi was mass produced in the early 70s and carried the connotations of computers today – adult and masculine. Though technical advances replaced reel-to-reel tape with cassettes and technology made hi-fi equipment, excluding speakers, ever smaller, the space it occupied was the 70s equivalent of the billiard room, a male preserve, often separated from the family. That said, teenagers' bedrooms also became private domains decorated with posters and filled with hi-fi equipment.

An important feature of the consumption of technology was its regular replacement. Finishes moved from a range of colours early in the 70s, through silver, to black by the end of the decade.

ILLUSTRATION 1
The House Book, Terence Conran, 1974

Photographer: John Donat © RIBA

ILLUSTRATION 1 The 70s marked the beginning of the period of extensions to houses, in part brought on by house price inflation. As well as the granny flat, the most common extensions were attic conversions and the construction of mezzanines, often in flats, accessed by prefabricated parts, including space-saving spiral stairs.

ILLUSTRATION 2 This giant Dieffenbachia is representative of the enormous popularity of large individual and groups of lush variegated-leaved houseplants in the early to mid 70s. In the later 70s, however, they fell from fashion and, where they were still used, it was on a much reduced scale.

Reproduced courtesy of Crossline plc manufacturers of the Hostess range 2006

ILLUSTRATION 3

Advertisement from Ideal Home, *September 1975*

ILLUSTRATION 3 With the advent of the open plan kitchen-dining room, the hostess trolley became one of those items of a middle-class household that was increasingly redundant. It represented the outmoded social world of the hostess in the kitchen – out of sight until presenting a meal, like a rabbit out of a hat. Increasingly in the 70s cooking was becoming part of the theatre of the dinner party. Given its transitory status, between cooking utensil and dining room furniture, it isn't surprising that its styling was part stainless steel, part 'teak' furniture, though by 1975 this was a very conservative style.

ILLUSTRATION 4 Though designed in the 60s, this case for the electric bell mechanism became a classic of the well detailed home throughout the 70s. Like the equally timeless Braun alarm clock, it lay below the threshold of what was considered interior design and thus escaped the judgement of fashion.

Reproduced courtesy of Honeywell International inc.

ILLUSTRATION 5

The Architectural Review, March 1975

Reproduced courtesy of The Architectural Review

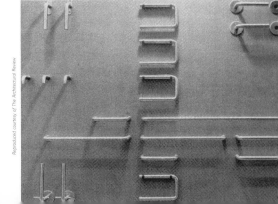

ILLUSTRATION 6
Homes and Gardens, May 1972

ILLUSTRATION 5 With the chunkier Modric range, designed in the 60s, the slimmer D-Line became a ubiquitous choice in architect-designed homes and interiors of the 70s as it offered co-ordinated designs for any architectural ironmongery task. However, in more fashion-conscious interiors, the eclecticism of the 70s led to revivals in the use of older door furniture in particular, and this kind of Modernist design became associated more with offices than homes.

ILLUSTRATION 6 With the increase in consumerism, homes became an increasing focus of what is elsewhere termed accessorisation. In the 70s by far the most luxurious, expensive and gestural addition to a home was a swimming pool. Though expensive they were, by comparison with earlier decades, cheaper and easier to install thanks to new materials and prefabrication. Their conspicuous glamour suited the mood of the early 70s well.

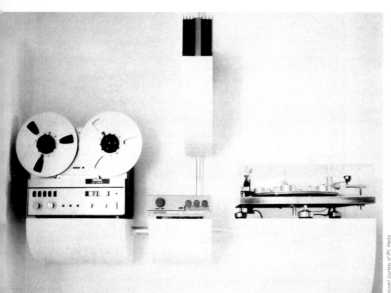

ILLUSTRATION 7
Homes and Gardens, *November 1974*

ILLUSTRATIONS 7, 8 & 9 Although unisex design was a feature of 70s fashion in the home, men still liked to design special spaces and things for themselves which emphasised 'manly' areas like technology and work. While there were ever fewer studies, there were other spaces like dining rooms or secondary living areas that could be given over to male pursuits. Arcane features of these areas were letter racks and desk tidies given fashionable makeovers by German or Italian designers. More important than signifiers of work were those of technology, particularly TVs with a high design content and small size; also elaborate stereo systems made up of different parts from different manufacturers. Only Bang and Olufsen managed to produce a really desirable unified hi-fi system based on the low profiles of the then fashionable sofas and coffee tables.

ILLUSTRATION 8
Homes and Gardens, *February 1977*
Desk tidy and Guzzini letter rack in plastic

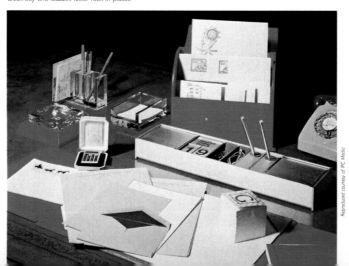

ILLUSTRATION 9

Homes and Gardens, *November 1974*

Reproduced courtesy of Denby UK

ILLUSTRATION 10

Advertisement from Ideal Home, September 1975

ILLUSTRATION 10 One solution to the effect of more relaxed lifestyles and new cleaning technologies on the pottery industry, was the development of oven-to-tableware. Though it existed in the 50s and 60s, it was ubiquitous by the 70s. Denby, who had always produced good simple kitchenware that was also oven-to-tableware, moved away from their rather utilitarian 'cottagey' designs in plain colours, and introduced ranges that followed fashions in furnishing fabrics.

ILLUSTRATION 11

Argos catalogue, 1977

Reproduced courtesy of Argos

ILLUSTRATION 11 Whereas in the early 60s stainless steel was an educated, design-conscious taste choice – by the 70s, with the development of consumerism, it was a mainstream choice. While in the 70s there was much eclectic experimentation with new styles amongst 'tastemakers', much of the population was still enjoying the access to the up-market taste of the 60s that consumerism was making available to them.

KITCHENS

Technical innovations included the introduction of the microwave cooker, glass-ceramic 'cooktops', tumble dryers and the synthetic stone material 'Corian', sold by DuPont from 1972. Existing technologies became more affordable and kitchen units were offered with a variety of specialised interiors, into which 'white goods' were designed to fit.

In the 70s, the kitchen came to represent idealised attitudes to the relationship between cooking and the home. At its root was the idea of the kitchen as a family room, which had the effect of making kitchens bigger and more decorative. In style these ranged from nostalgic historicism to a generalised wholesomeness. While the farmhouse idea dominated the market, gentrified city homes had basements converted into a take on the servants' kitchen. As decor became more mood-oriented, units became available in finishes that accommodated these 'themes', as did kitchen equipment. Pans, mugs, breadbins and chopping boards carried depictions of small animals, birds and stalks of wheat, often in the browns and beiges which dominated the middle-range designs of the decade. Utility rooms were increasingly used to house appliances that detracted from the kitchen as a 'themed' room.

In the early 70s there was a parallel fashion for kitchens in strong oranges and yellows. In architect-designed homes there was a concurrent fashion for Brutalist 'engineered' finishes, primary colours and an industrial layout. This aesthetic reappeared in modified form in the late 70s with the more metallic, high-tech style of Richard Rogers and Michael Hopkins.

Towards the end of the 70s, there was a reaction against prefabricated units and the tight, work-efficient layout of cooking areas. One reaction was the creation of kitchen-dining rooms, with a minimal approach to the layout of units and cookers. Another was the reverse, a taste for elaborate, handmade kitchens, built around professional equipment. The island unit was popular for expensive kitchens throughout the decade.

ILLUSTRATION 1

The House Book, *Terence Conran, 1974*

ILLUSTRATION 2

Advertisement from House and Garden,
December & January 1975-76

ILLUSTRATION 1 In many 70s homes, the kitchen became incorporated into the reception rooms. It was no longer a segregated place of hygienic food preparation but rather the central point in the 'theatre' of food. The island kitchen suited this new role as it could be placed like a capsule toward one end of a dining room that was decorated like a living room.

ILLUSTRATION 3
Advertisement from House and
Garden, July & August 1975

ILLUSTRATION 2 This is a very typical 70s kitchen at the upper end of the middle market – large, bland, practical and well appointed with a separate inset electric hob and oven. The mustard colour scheme was one of the most popular of the decade and could be found on many household products from pans to Hoovers and even on Leyland cars.

ILLUSTRATION 3 Although the advertisement claims this is a 'dream kitchen', plenty like it were built. Its design shows how far people had moved from practical considerations dominating kitchen design. Here, the kitchen combines elements of the dining room and the bedroom – the dining bar looking like a dressing table, not least because the units around it are made from redwood-toned louvred doors that were a common feature in fitted bedroom furniture of the period. Note the influence of 'glam Deco' styling on the fridge and oven doors.

ILLUSTRATION 4

Advertisement from House and Garden, *November 1973*

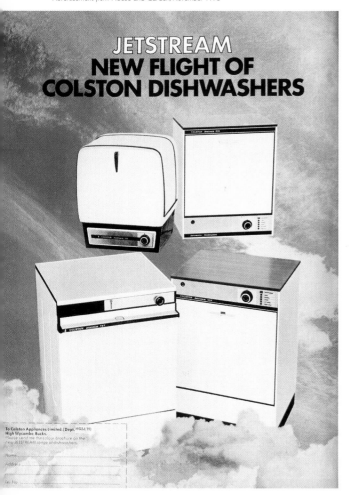

JETSTREAM
NEW FLIGHT OF
COLSTON DISHWASHERS

ILLUSTRATION 4 As consumerism increased, the technology of convenience became boring to homeowners. A desire to hide appliances away from view led to the production of more 'hideable' dishwashers than the tabletop versions which were typical of the 60s. Microwaves, new in the 1970s, received the same tabletop treatment that dishwashers had previously enjoyed.

ILLUSTRATION 5 Throughout the 70s dark brown was a popular colour for cookers and ovens. Brown was the 'warm' alternative to the self-effacing grey and black used in other rooms by goods from Sony and Braun. The wall-mounted double fan oven with glass front has become a standard design for these goods and shares with the microwave a debt to the visual compositions of television design. Note the non-LED digital timer that typified the 1970s clock.

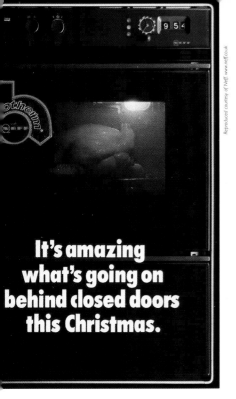

It's amazing what's going on behind closed doors this Christmas.

ILLUSTRATION 5

Advertisement from House and Garden,
December & January 1978-79

If you could choose what you'd really want, Miele is what you'd buy.

Miele is expensive. Something that makes
But the best usually is. the rich, idle.
It's the price of excellence And the idle, rich.
and exclusivity.

ILLUSTRATION 6

Advertisement from House and Garden, *April 1973*

ILLUSTRATION 6 In the 70s the variety and consumption of domestic appliances increased. In their traditional home in the kitchen, their bulk and noise began to interfere with the increasing use of kitchen areas as social spaces for family and guests, as well as with fashionable kitchen styles like the 'farmhouse' or 'below stairs' kitchen. The solution to this problem was the creation of the utility room where noisy appliances like washing machines and tumble dryers and large appliances like chest freezers could be housed – in effect creating a modern service technology room that combined the roles of the old larder and scullery, which in old houses were often converted to this use.

Two large hotplates. One fast-boiling, the other slow and gentle – for that exotic sauce!

And the same with Aga's two large ovens. One for roasting and baking, the other for slow gentle cooking.

An Aga kitchen is warm and welcoming.

An Aga stores its heat to give even, all-over cooking.

Aga heat is controlled to ensure that flavour and juices are sealed in.

The Exotic Black Aga, with copper fittings.

ILLUSTRATION 7

Advertisement from Homes and Gardens, *October 1974*

ILLUSTRATION 8

Eleanor Greeves ceramic tile, 1971

ILLUSTRATION 7 Along with Le Creuset pan sets, Aga ranges became the most desirable kitchen features of the 70s. What was a functional kitchen feature in the 50s was transformed into the centrepiece of a celebration of the domestic, as kitchens became a key site of self-expression. The Aga company responded to this new fashionability by producing its ranges in a number of strong colours rather than the old-fashioned black, white and cream.

ILLUSTRATION 8 A typical 70s pattern in a typical 70s colour. The revival in interest in the arts and crafts led to patterns which took as their inspiration designers like Morris and De Morgan, and in particular the ethos of clear naturalism, rendered in a manner that makes 'printedness' apparent. In kitchens, tiles like these were often interspersed with plain tiles around stoves or along splash-backs. The popularity of this sort of design in the kitchen declined toward the end of the decade as, although based on old design ideas, their screen print technique and thin glaze and tile made them look too recently modern.

FIREPLACES AND HEATING

The oil crisis and coal strikes of the early 70s made oil and electricity expensive compared to the new fuel, natural gas. Equally, the creation of 'smokeless zones' in domestic areas after the Clean Air Act in 1968 greatly reduced the use of coal for heating. These factors meant gas-fired systems gradually emerged as the dominant form of central heating in the 1970s. In 1971, 34 per cent of homes had central heating, whereas in 1983 this figure had increased to 64 per cent.

Hot water radiators replaced technologically advanced systems installed in the 60s like underfloor electric heating or hot air pumped through ducts. In some homes, cheap night-supply electric storage radiators were fitted. In new houses double glazing became more frequently fitted and homes were better insulated through the use of foam-filled cavity walls and roof insulation.

As domestic heating became more taken for granted there was, perversely, a revival in the use and installation of fires. Young homeowners moving into the old inner-city suburbs in the early 70s treated fireplaces as part of the architecture, frequently retaining the surround but removing the grate, plastering the hole and decorating the result as part of the room.

As the decade progressed there were the beginnings of a restoration culture first pioneered in the pages of The Architectural Review. By the end of the decade architectural salvage companies had started to satisfy the demand for old fireplaces. They were fuelled most often by wood, which was seen as 'nicer' than coal, although early gas log and gas coal systems existed. In the country and the homes of ecologically inclined city dwellers, Scandinavian wood-burning stoves became popular.

New houses designed by architects almost always featured a big open wood fire whereas speculative developments rarely had any provision for them, so having a fire became a status symbol. Equally, Aga stoves powered by gas rather than coal or oil appeared on the market. These became a sort-after luxury in gentrified homes whilst the Rayburn was popular in smaller country homes.

ILLUSTRATION 2
The House Book, Terence Conran, 1974

ILLUSTRATION 1
Advertisement from Ideal Home, January 1975

The Main Richmond Gas Fire

The closest you'll ever get to a real log fire.

ILLUSTRATION 1 The gas fire was a feature of many homes and flats from the late 50s onwards. Traditionally a rather basic device in the living room of average households, by the mid 70s manufacturers had begun to recognise the increasing selectivity of consumers who would no longer settle for functionalism. Here, in recognition of the growing demand for 'real' fires, the manufacturer has attempted to convert the gas fire into an easily installed, miniaturised version of the open log fire so common on the continent.

ILLUSTRATION 2 Stoves became an increasingly popular way to bring the humanising influence of fire into homes that were left a little too sanitised by the ubiquitous background heat of central heating. Their simple and freestanding form made them easy to combine with many styles of decor though usually people who liked stoves favoured the eclectic.

ILLUSTRATION 3
Advertisement from Homes and Gardens, *November 1972*

ILLUSTRATION 3 Fires were an obvious focus for the historicism that emerged in the 70s, as seen in this Baxi Burnall advertisement of 1972. However, fireplaces were more commonly reopened and reused in combination with modern furnishings and this easy, undoctrinaire mixture of old and new was a significant development of 70s interior design.

ILLUSTRATION 4
Advertisement from House and Garden, *February 1973*

ILLUSTRATION 4 The Baxi fire was the last gasp of the coal fire. It was designed around an underfloor supply of air to the base of the fire and was the most high-tech open fire on the market. This advertisement, placed at the time of the oil crisis and followed by coal strikes, was a desperate attempt to maintain the falling demand for coal fires. The Baxi's main problem was that it was too small to burn wood well or to look good as a free-standing fire, like those being designed by contemporary architects.

Reproduced courtesy of Baxi Heating UK

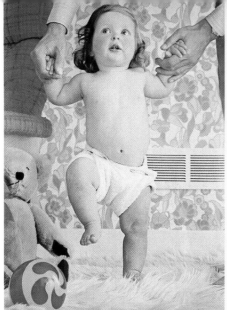

Overnight, Susan's Daddy found he could afford electric central heating

Enjoy an 'overnight success'—like Susan's Daddy—simply by going to White Meter for all your electricity! The White Meter supplies all electricity used overnight at half price. The electricity you use during the day is at one price, but the electricity you use during the night is half that price! So people who use electricity overnight for storage water heating and Electricaire central heating can really make big economies on their electricity bill.

ELECTRICAIRE
is being built into more new houses every year. This electric central heating system works from a central unit which can go under the stairs or into a cupboard. It stores up heat mainly overnight, when electricity is half-price on the White Meter, to keep the house warm during the day. Built-in ducts waft warm air to each room through small grilles at skirting level or in the floor. Once installed, the system is entirely automatic. You have no fuel storage problems, and no fumes or dirty flues to worry about. And it's easy to afford on the White Meter!

STORAGE WATER HEATING
The hot water for your daily needs is mainly heated at half-price on the White Meter, overnight, then stored for use in a properly insulated tank which keeps the water really hot until you want it. The water heating is, of course, independent of the central heating so you don't have to run a boiler during the summer!

EASY TO AFFORD
The White Meter records daytime electricity at one price, and then switches itself automatically to overnight electricity—for *everything* that uses it—at half that price! On top of that, remember your electricity board offers budget payment plans which enable you to spread running costs evenly over the year. So it all becomes easy to afford. Ask for details...and enjoy an overnight success!

White Meter brings you half-price electricity OVERNIGHT!

ILLUSTRATION 5

Advertisement from House and Garden, *September 1971*

ILLUSTRATION 6

The House Book, Terence Conran, *1974*

Photographer: Jerry Tubby

ILLUSTRATION 5 This advertisement for electric heating shows a pumped hot air system, Electricaire, based on stored heat produced from cheap night-time electricity. What these systems saved in space they made up for in installation costs and average heating performance. Moreover, people were unconvinced by arguments based on pricing in a time of constant inflation. The 70s, though it saw a 30 per cent increase in centrally heated homes, was marked by technological conservatism driven by price. Radiators have remained an interior decor problem ever since.

ILLUSTRATION 6 This shows an old coal fireplace that has had its surround and fireback removed to reveal the basic fireplace cavity. This is large enough to house a wood fire which was far more desirable to the 70s homemaker than coal. This kind of conversion to wood from coal was common as it was easy and looked modern. As in this case, the hearth often had to be raised to get the wood to burn properly or to prevent the room filling with smoke. Wood-burning stoves inserted into old fireplaces avoided these problems altogether.

BATHROOMS

Bathrooms were the rooms most transformed by the tastes of the 70s, ceasing to be purely functional and becoming places of private luxury and contemplation. Not only did they become more luxurious, they increased in scale and, by the end of the decade, were far more numerous per household.

In new bathrooms of the early 70s it was fashionable to place the bath in the centre of the room, sometimes on a pedestal. Generally, though, bathroom equipment was conventionally positioned around the perimeter of the room. What changed most was the decoration and quantity of equipment.

Both steel and the new acrylic baths took on colours that followed the fashions of fabrics. In the early 70s, architect-designed bathrooms would use very dark colours, blue and red suites contrasted with oranges and yellows in the tiled walls. Faucets and door fittings were also available in brightly coloured plastic. Tiles were often matt oblongs or small terrazzo tile sheets. In bathrooms with a skylight or no natural light, mirror-tiled walls were popular; with floors tiled in white. This style remained popular right into the 80s with architects who continued to design small bathrooms.

Designs were much more lavish. The decade began with bathrooms that evoked luxury through materials and abundance of facilities and ended with rooms that evoked the historic styles of principal rooms. In restored houses it was popular to try and preserve original fittings like roll-top baths.

The mid-range bathroom entered the 70s in sombre colours, most famously 'avocado', which was later joined by the equally famous 'whisper peach' along with dark brown and beige. Towels were sold to co-ordinate with these colours. The main innovations in equipment were bidets, vanity units, invisible plumbing, oval corner baths and wall-to-wall carpet. The shapes of suites were based on rectangles or ovals while fittings were often chunky and flat-sided. It was also fashionable to have 'his and hers' basins and, in architect-designed houses, a child's bathroom with lowered suites.

ILLUSTRATION I

The Hopkins House, 1976, Hampstead

ILLUSTRATION I This bathroom is in the high-tech style of the mid and late 70s. The bathroom is a free standing prefabricated module within the house and this recalls the radical Italian design of the early 70s as does its stark simplicity and use of overtly prefabricated and plastic elements. The reduction of the toilet and shower and their

ILLUSTRATION 2
The House Book, Terence Conran, 1974

© Camera Press

ILLUSTRATION 3
The House Book, Terence Conran, 1974

© Camera Press

attendant controls to a minimal presence in the room is an extreme version of a tendency in most modernist 70s bathrooms. It is also an early example of a wet room. Though in Britain this type of design was overshadowed by the historicist revival of the late 70s and 80s, it was popular in European interiors.

ILLUSTRATIONS 2 & 3 As bathrooms became a major feature of the home so they also became more interestingly designed, using imagery and forms taken from furniture design. Here Illustration 2 shows the influence of total furniture or environment furniture in the design of this room as one surface that can be moved around to undertake a number of activities. The use of textured sponge rubber shows the influence of avant-garde Italian furniture. Illustration 3 shows the influence of Italian capsule furniture in its use of industrial materials and the design, which maximises use in a minimum of space.

ILLUSTRATION 5

Advertisement from Homes and Gardens, *July 1974*

ILLUSTRATION 4

Advertisement from House and Garden, *November 1973*

There is now a ceramic tile which matches up to Amtico vinyl tiles.

ILLUSTRATION 4 Amtico were an early producer of luxury tiles in vinyl and in the mid 70s they introduced a range of ceramic wall tiles to meet the demand for co-ordination in bathrooms and kitchens. These bright complex patterned tiles with a reversed-out contrast between walls and floors show the 70s notion of co-ordination well and the pattern, with its fairly hispanic feel, represents the way in which the 70s used pattern to reference other cultures with intentional vagueness.

ILLUSTRATION 5 The vanity unit was to the 70s what the en suite bathroom became in the 90s. Vanity units were essentially dressing tables with washbasins set into them. They became a standard feature in bathrooms and many master bedrooms, where the wide range of coloured basins and more decorative taps than were available

ILLUSTRATION 7

A Hampstead bathroom decorated with Eleanor Greeves
'Marigold' tiles, from the artist's album of commissions, June 1974

BADDA 4095

in the 60s meant that vanity units could easily be made to fit in with bedroom decor.

ILLUSTRATION 6 Though a shower over the bath remained a very common solution, more bathrooms had separate shower cubicles in the 70s which came with efficient sealing doors allowing the bathroom to remain dry and warm – dry enough for bathroom shag pile carpet. In the 1970s, bathrooms emphasised warmth and dryness to contrast with memories of cold air and slippery floors from 60s bathrooms.

ILLUSTRATION 7 A typical middle-class bathroom at the turn of the decade; despite cork floor tiles and pretty Morris revival tiles, the bathroom remains a tidy necessity. Note the typical treatment of the hot water tank airing cupboard at the rear of the room.

If you're going to splash out, make sure you do it in the bathroom.

It is now possible to indulge yourself with a bathroom as luxurious, as stylish, as immaculately furnished as the remainder of your abode.

With the addition of what are, quite simply, the most beautiful water fittings obtainable.

Created by Deltaflow (the United Kingdom's most significant producer of such items), the bath/shower unit pictured here is finished in 22 carat gold plate, and has headworks which are sculptured from solid onyx marble.

It costs about as much as a reasonable television set. The Golden Onyx range is augmented by basin, and bidet taps and mixers, so that each piece of porcelain can reflect similar splendour. Matching accessories are also available. You know the sort of thing... imaginative little baubles like solid onyx tumblers, gold plated towel rails, shelves which combine both these materials.

The usual ephemera of decadence, in fact...

And if all this should be just a little too much, we also have fittings sculptured in more traditional chrome, but also with onyx heads—this time of a pinkish hue.

Someone recently opined that when Mr Healey said 'Soak the rich', this is what he meant.

See the Deltaflow Gold and Onyx and Silver and Onyx ranges at your local stockist. Or, for our opulent full colour brochure, write to Deltaflow Limited, Dept, D133, 14/16 Windmill Road, Hampton Hill, Middlesex.

ILLUSTRATION 8

Advertisement from House and Garden, *December & January 1978-79*

ILLUSTRATION 10

Advertisement from Homes and Gardens, *October 1974*

ILLUSTRATION 9

Advertisement from House and Garden, *December & January 1978-79*

ILLUSTRATIONS 8 & 9 As the advertisement says, you can now furnish your bathroom to the same luxurious standard as the rest of your home. Presaging the 'greed is good' years of the 80s, gold-plated taps became notorious (if not popular) in the late 70s. These models have real onyx knobs and also came with a range of co-ordinated hangers, rails and soap dishes. Chrome models were available with pink onyx knobs.

Note the modern dark suite in a 'Victorian' setting which is not as contrived as it may appear.

ILLUSTRATION 10 As bathrooms became imbued with the aura of luxury rather than hygiene, bath design took on a more Roman aspect. The idea behind the corner bath and the reason why, even in beige, it was considered a bit risqué, was that it was designed to contain two people and was not solely for washing.

ILLUSTRATION 11
Advertisement from Homes and Gardens, *May 1972*

ILLUSTRATION 11 The ultimate moderately well off 70s bathroom: WC and bidet with matching extra-size tissue holder and towel holders, bath with shower attachment, all in avocado with gold-plated fittings and accessories.

ILLUSTRATION 12 This bathroom in Flamingo, a re-release of a colour popular in the USA in the 50s, shows the innovations to bathroom layout that occurred in the 70s. The bath is moved off the wall and into the room; there is a separate shower with a 150cm tray, larger than the old 100cm trays; toilet and bidet are placed together but away from the bath and the his and hers washbasins. Men were now beginning to take long self-indulgent baths!

ILLUSTRATION 12
Advertisement from House and Garden, *April 1975*

FURTHER READING

The House Book
Terence Conran (1974)

Decorative Art 70s
Charlotte and Peter Fiell, eds (2000)

The 70s House
David Heathcote (2005)
Photography by Sue Barr

Interior Desecrations: Hideous Homes
from the Horrible Seventies
James Lileks (2004)

Barbican: Penthouse Over the City
David Heathcote (2004)
Photography by Sue Barr

The 1970s is Here and Now
(*Architectural Design*, April 2005)
Samantha Hardingham, ed.

Sixtiestyle
David Heathcote (2004)

PLACES TO VISIT

MoDA (The Museum of Domestic Design & Architecture), Middlesex University, Cat Hill, Barnet, Hertfordshire EN4 8HT Telephone 020 8411 5244 www.moda.mdx.ac.uk
MoDA's collections of trade catalogues, home magazines, designs, wallpapers and textiles can be viewed by appointment in MoDA's study room.

THE BARBICAN ESTATE AND WINTER GARDEN, preserved apartment, the Barbican, City of London
The Barbican Arts Centre and Estate are full of good examples of 70s design including some of the garden spaces. There is a proposal to make a heritage apartment open to the public as the residential buildings are now listed.

KETTLE'S YARD, Castle Street, Cambridge CB3 0AQ Telephone 01223 352124 www.kettlesyard.co.uk
In 1956 Jim and Helen Ede, with the help of architect Roland Aldridge, restored and substantially remodelled four tumbledown cottages, making them into a domestic space where paintings and sculpture are interlaced with furniture, glass, ceramics and natural objects. In 1970 it was considerably extended in an uncompromisingly contemporary style by Sir Leslie Martin and David Owers. The house and the Ede's collections of Modern art and antique furnishings reflect a uniquely British and romantic response to Modernism and heritage – it is in effect a contemporary stately home. Within the confines of this small property it is possible to read the development of the modern interior from the 50s to the 70s.

LITTLE SPARTA, the garden of Ian Hamilton Finlay, Little Sparta Trust, Stonypath, Dunsyre, Nr Lanark, South Lanarkshire, Scotland Telephone 01556 640244
Though begun in the late 1960s, the poet Ian Hamilton Finlay's garden really only began to develop through the 70s. It is a unique mixture of poetry, sculpture, philosophy and politics and has been described as "the only really original garden made in this country since 1945".

THE 1970S GARDEN, RHS HARLOW CARR GARDENS, Crag Lane, Harrogate, North Yorkshire HG3 1QB Telephone 01423 565418
The RHS has created a number of gardens at Harlow Carr representing the recent history of gardens. Their 70s garden focuses on, amongst other things, the garden as extension of the house. This key element in many 70s town gardens was achieved through the creation of an outside room using patios, pergolas and evergreen planting.

MoDA is known as the 'museum of the history of the home'. Its varied exhibitions give a vivid picture of domestic life during the first half of the twentieth century whilst also looking at contemporary design and other issues related to the domestic environment.

Gallery talks, events, practical workshops and study days provide educational, informative and entertaining experiences for adults and children.

MoDA holds six collections and a dedicated Study Room allows access to items not on display.

SILVER STUDIO COLLECTION

The archive of a commercial pattern design practice active between 1880 and 1963. Its many thousands of designs, wallpapers and textile samples span the popular styles of the period.

CROWN WALLPAPER COLLECTION

Wallpaper books mainly from the 1950s, represent the colourful and engaging patterns of that time.

DOMESTIC DESIGN COLLECTION

More than 4,000 books, magazines and trade catalogues relating to design for the home and household management (1850-1960).

SIR JM RICHARDS LIBRARY

Books and journals collected by Sir JM Richards (1907-1992), a leading architectural writer. The collection covers architecture, interiors, furniture, landscape and town planning.

PEGGY ANGUS ARCHIVE

The entire contents of the London studio of Peggy Angus (1904-1993), an artist, teacher and designer of tiles and bespoke hand-printed wallpapers.

CHARLES HASLER COLLECTION

An archive relating to the work of Charles Hasler (1908-1992), a typographer and graphic designer who played a significant role in many high-profile exhibitions, poster campaigns and in book publishing from the mid-1930s to the mid-1980s.